HOW TO DRAW
GHOSTS, GOBLINS,
and WITCHES
AND OTHER *SPOOKY* CHARACTERS

Written and Illustrated by **Barbara Soloff-Levy**

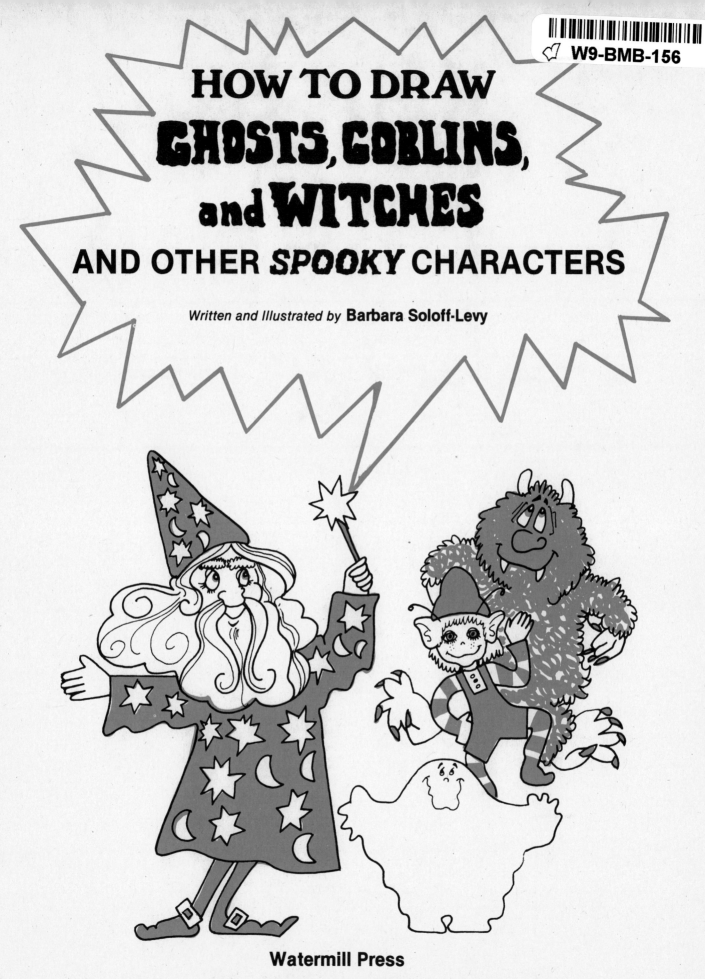

Watermill Press

MATERIALS

Quarter

Coins
or anything round
You'll use them to draw circles (or just practice drawing circles and do them freehand).

Half dollar

Pencils

Number 2 pencils are best for drawing. You should have at least three of them.

Crayons
or
Markers

You will need a set of crayons or colored markers. If you choose markers, get a medium-size flat point or a bullet point.

White Paper

A 9″ × 12″ pad of drawing paper or typing paper can be used.

DRAWING PAD

Felt-Tip Pens

You will need at least two. These will be used to do your final drawing.

Ruler

For drawing straight lines.

Eraser

HOW TO DRAW:
AN INTRODUCTION

An artist never draws a final picture on the first try. A drawing is something that grows, step by step, as you work. Here is an easy way to draw your spooky characters.

Begin your picture by drawing the basic shapes shown in Step 1. Draw them lightly in pencil. Add to your drawing, as shown in Step 2. Then add the final details shown in Step 3.

You can now go over your pencil drawing with a felt-tip pen. Erase any unwanted pencil lines, and then color your spooky character.

Of course, you can change the eyes, ears, or whatever you like to make your drawing look the way you want it to. Remember, *you* are the artist—and the most important thing is to have fun as you draw!

Step 1   **Step 2**   **Step 3**

GHOSTS

There are all types of ghosts—friendly, scary, tricky, and mean ones. Some folks say ghosts were once people that became spirits. You'll usually find ghosts in haunted houses and castles.

1

2

3

1

2

3

AND MORE GHOSTS

1

Ghosts love to trick people. They can become invisible or take on any shape or form. That's why they're so much fun to draw!

2

1

2

Some funny faces to try

3

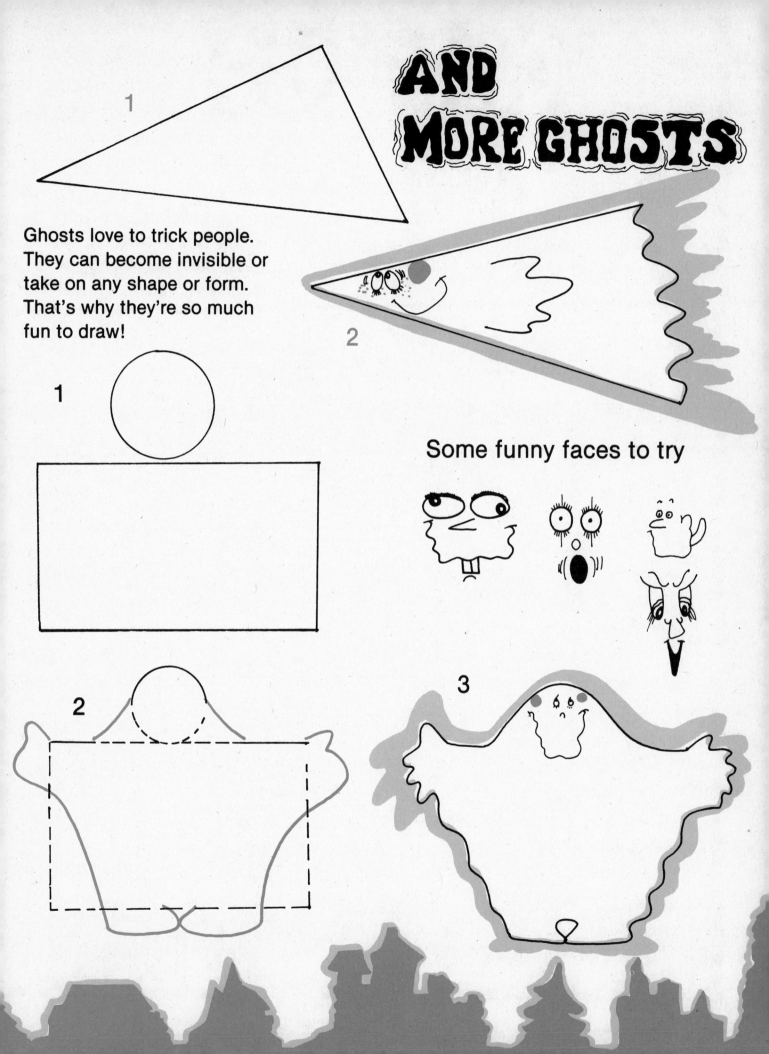

WITCH

MEAN WITCH

Witches have magical powers. This is a mean witch. She loves to cook bubbling "Witches' Brew" in her caldron.

1

2

3

4

5

6

WITCH

GOOD WITCH

1

2

3

8

4

For every wicked witch, there is also a good witch. Good witches use their magical powers to make things better. This good witch has a pet cat. All witches have magical brooms, which they use for sweeping floors and for flying through the sky on dark Halloween nights.

5

Notice the detail on the face.

9

OGRE

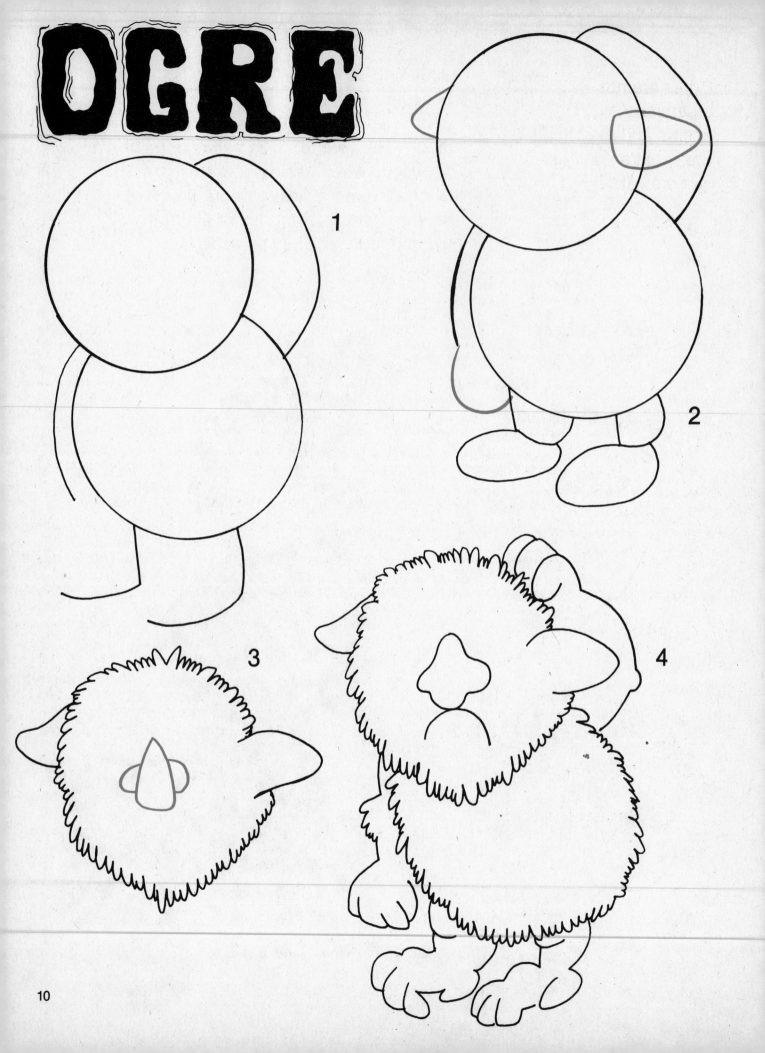

1

2

3

4

Ogres are not very handsome
creatures. They love to scare
people and play tricks on
them. Let's see how mean you
can draw this ogre.

5

Try these silly
faces, also.

GOBLIN

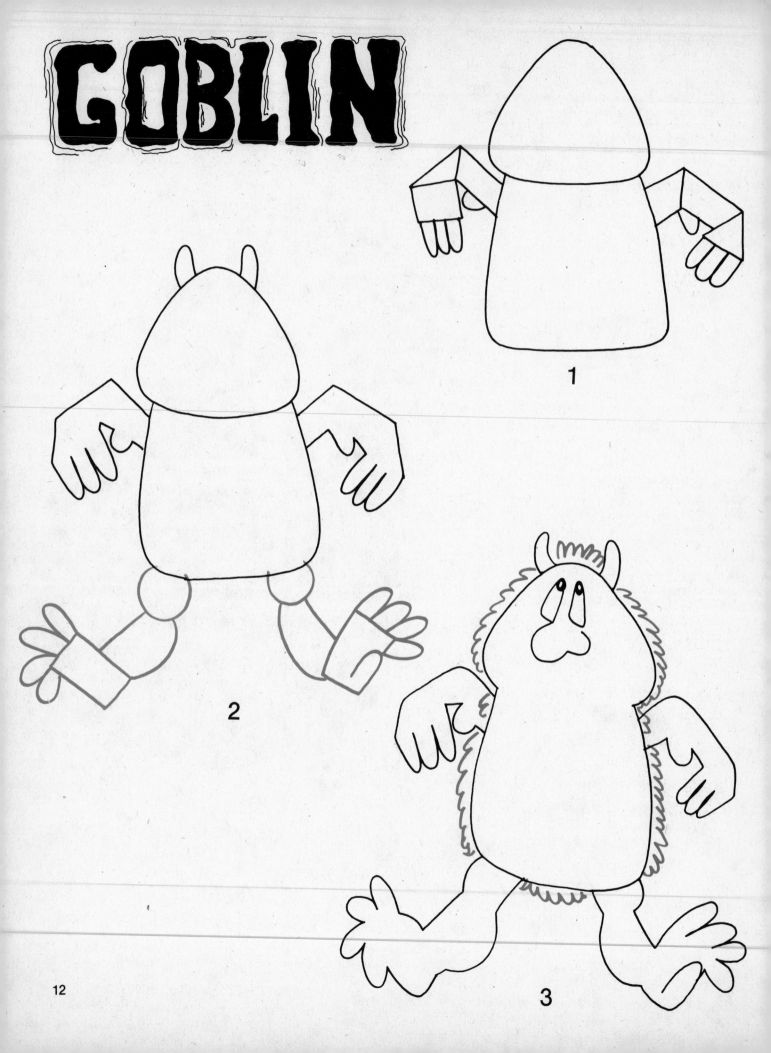

1

2

3

4

Here are two more faces you might like to try.

Goblins are nasty little creatures, full of mischief. Often they sneak up and scare you—especially in the dark. They have horns on their heads and lots of hair. They use their long nails to scratch along the blackboard!

5

13

HAUNTED HOUSE

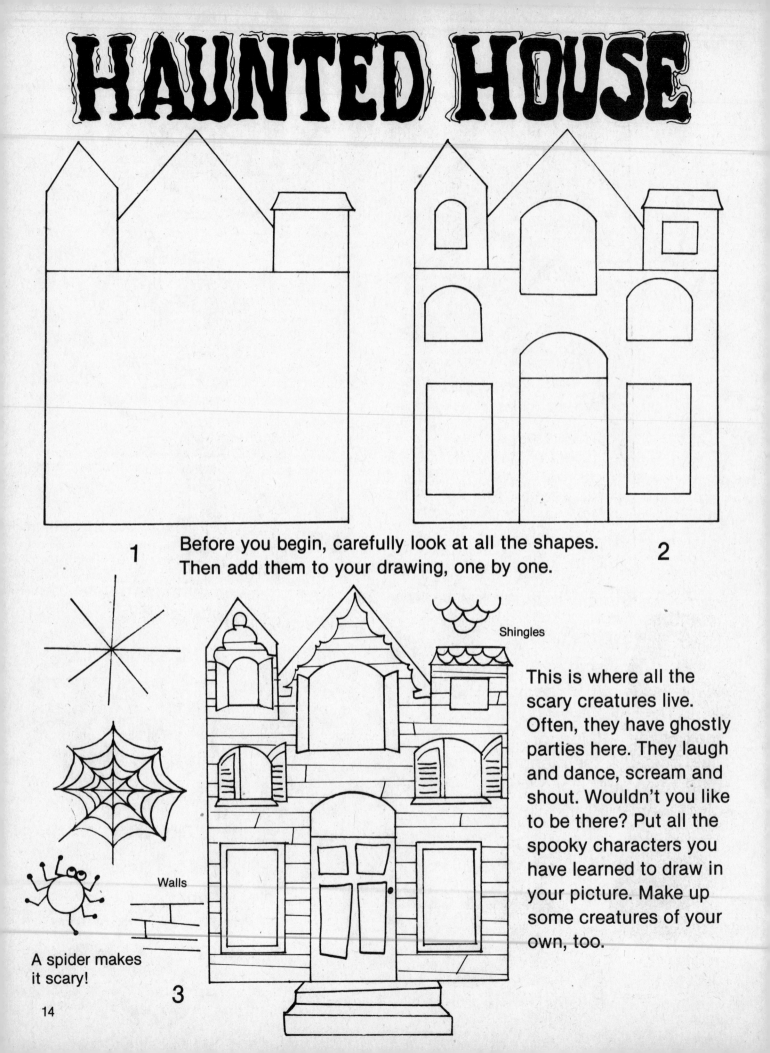

1

Before you begin, carefully look at all the shapes. Then add them to your drawing, one by one.

2

Shingles

Walls

A spider makes it scary!

3

This is where all the scary creatures live. Often, they have ghostly parties here. They laugh and dance, scream and shout. Wouldn't you like to be there? Put all the spooky characters you have learned to draw in your picture. Make up some creatures of your own, too.

FAIRY

1

2

3

A fairy is a tiny creature with magical powers. This is a flower fairy. Dressed in flower petals, she loves to dance among the flowers. She lives in fairyland, a special place of enchantment. Of course, the flowers in her garden have magical powers. The primrose has the power to make fairies visible, and a four-leaf clover can break any spell.

4

5

ELF

1

2

3

18

Elves are carefree little people who live underground or high up in trees. They are extremely helpful and very playful. It's the elf who helps Santa at the North Pole, creating beautiful toys. It is also the elf who helps us find our way out of the forest.

4

5

PIXIE

1

2

3

4

Meet Peter the Pixie. He is a mischievous little fairy. Pixies love to dance in the shadows and ride upon insects. These little fairies don't fly. They just skip and prance about.

5

6

LEPRECHAUN

5

Ah! 'Tis true I am a leprechaun. I hoard all the gold I find at the end of the rainbow. I am tricky and sly, and can disappear with the wink of an eye. Color me green, if you wish.

6

GOLD

23

UNICORN

It isn't very often you'll see a unicorn. This magical beast looks like a horse with a spiral horn. The unicorn means good luck for you, if you can catch one! Unicorns are usually milky white. But go ahead and color yours any color you like.

1

2

3

4

5

25

DRAGON

1

2

3

4

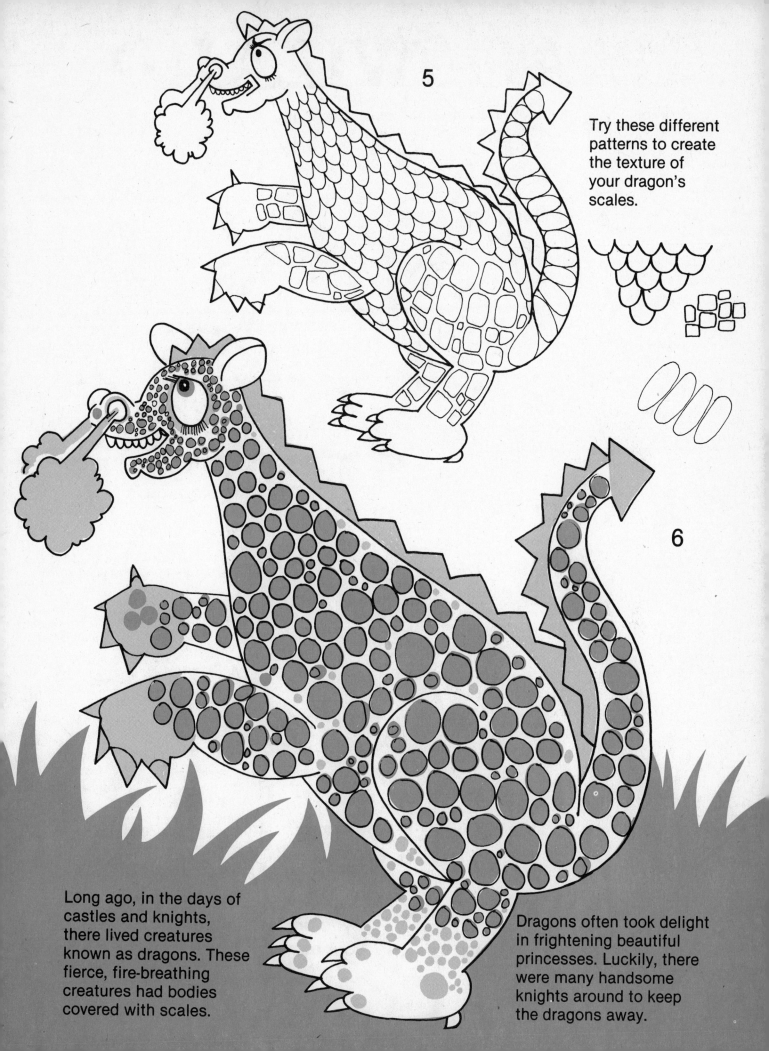

5

Try these different patterns to create the texture of your dragon's scales.

6

Long ago, in the days of castles and knights, there lived creatures known as dragons. These fierce, fire-breathing creatures had bodies covered with scales.

Dragons often took delight in frightening beautiful princesses. Luckily, there were many handsome knights around to keep the dragons away.

WIZARD

1

2

3

Try to draw this prince—*oops*—FROG! Study the basic shapes. Then try to draw one of your own.

4

Magic is my game! I can turn anybody into almost anything. I live in a castle, all by myself, and I spend most of my time thinking up all sorts of magical charms and spells. My favorite is to turn a handsome prince into a frog.

5

CASTLE

1

2

Castles are usually built out of stone so they're strong. Castles protect the people who live inside them from their enemies—like the fire-breathing dragon!

Just keep adding on, until you have a beautiful castle!

3

Here are some different patterns for drawing the castle's walls and roof.

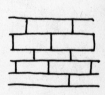

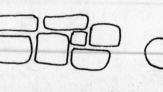

4

Make up your own fairy tale and draw it. Include the characters you have just learned to draw. Then create some of your own. Remember— in the magical world of charms and spells, anything can happen!

MY OWN STORY

Use this page to make up your very own story. It can be about ghosts, goblins, dragons, elves—or anything you like! Instead of using names, draw a picture of each character as you write your story.